# STAN
# AND ITS ANCIENT
# STONE CIRCLES

*Gordon Strong*

*To all those to whom I have unveiled this magical site, and in gratitude for the insights they have passed on to me.*

*Many thanks to Anthony, Arts Librarian at the Reference Library at Bristol Central Library for his help with the illustrations for this book, to Dan Goodfellow for his illustrations on pages 6, 34, 35 and 43, and to my editors and additional picture researchers John Martineau, Hugh Newman and Jon King.*

*H. M. J. Underhill's 1895 watercolour sketch of the small northeasterly circle at Stanton Drew*

# CONTENTS

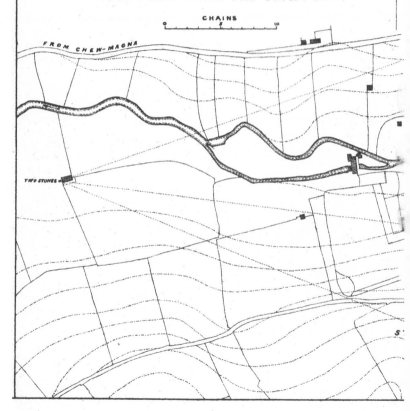

GENERAL PLAN

REDUCED FROM THE TITHE MAP.

CHAINS

FROM CHEW-MAGNA

TWO STONES

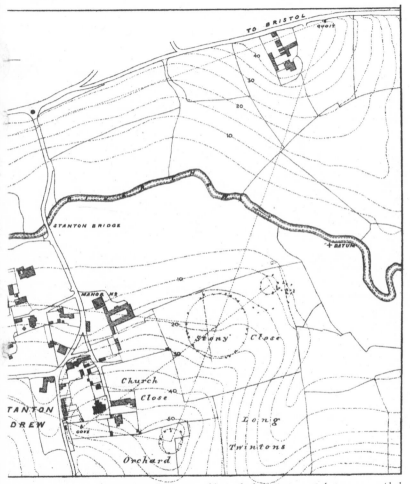

*C. W. Dymond's 1896 survey of the site, clearly showing two westerly stones, now vanished.*

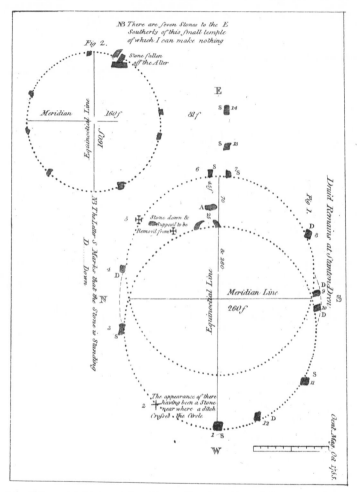

*A fanciful geometrical interpretation of Stanton Drew from the Gentleman's Magazine of 1785*

# INTRODUCTION

Stone circles are found throughout Great Britain and Europe, but only Avebury and Stonehenge top the magnificence of the triple stone circles of Stanton Drew in Somerset. Although little is known of this third great temple of southern England, it is true to say that modern techniques are at last beginning to unravel its ancient secrets. A 1997 English Heritage geophysical survey revealed that the stone circles are the remains of a far more elaborate site than was previously believed, with similar features to Woodhenge, and the Sanctuary near Avebury.

As with other Neolithic sites, the accurate astroarchaeological alignments of the sun and moon cycles suggest that the 'savages' who built these magnificent monuments were smarter than current preconceptions allow. At the same time, they remind us how the circles would have played an integral part in ancient social and religious life. Questions surrounding these issues, and others such as quite how such mighty stones were quarried, transported, positioned and erected, still baffle the modern engineer and remain some of the most elusive mysteries surrounding our ancient cousins.

What we do know is that the construction of stone monuments began around 3,500 BC and continued for over 2,000 years, marking a period when our forebears began more and more to settle, and thus to begin to erect more permanent structures. The virtually untouched megaliths of Stanton Drew might thus be viewed as a gateway to the lost knowledge of our West Country ancestors.

# THE AREA SURROUNDING
## *history and location*

The name Stanton Drew derives from the Old Saxon for Stone Town (*Stan-Ton*) and the fact that, during the Middle Ages, the land surrounding the stone circles was owned by the Drogo family, a Norman name which evolved into the Anglo–Celtic word for magician, sorcerer or druid '*Dru*', '*Dryw*', or more commonly today, '*Drew*'. Hence 'Stanton Drew', or 'Stone Town of the Drew Family'.

The Hauteville's were another powerful French noble family who settled in Somerset and the West Country in the 11th and 12th centuries and held the manor at Stanton Drew. Tancred, Sire de Hauteville, was courtier to Richard II, and Roger de Stanton, descendant of Tancred, owned the manor of Stanton Drew at Domesday (circa 1086 AD).

*Petrosomatoglyphs on the Pool Farm cist cover (from north of Priddy, Somerset)*

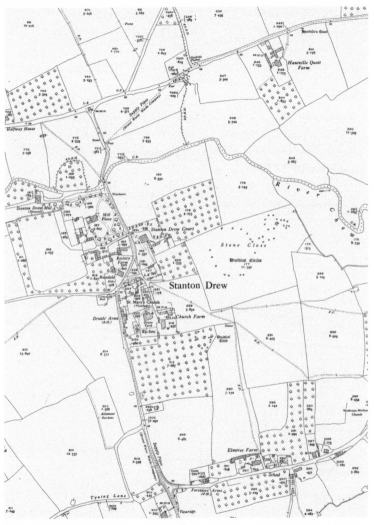

Stanton Drew

# EARLY PLANS
## antiquarian maps and surveys

The circles at Stanton Drew were first noted by the 17th century antiquarian, John Aubrey, in 1664. At about the same time, a Mr. John Wood visited Stanton Drew and made a plan of the site, but his visit was accompanied by a storm and the villagers accused him of having 'Disturbed the Guardian Spirit of the metamorphosed stones.'

In 1776, the first comprehensive drawings of the stones were made by William Stukeley (*next page*), who believed the site comprised part of a sacred pattern with centres at Stonehenge and Avebury.

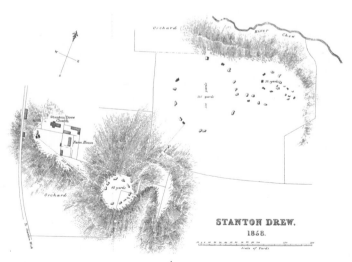

STANTON DREW.
1858.

Scale of Yards

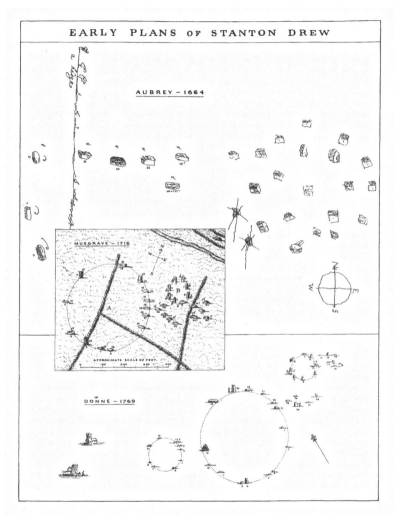

# EARLY PLANS of STANTON DREW

AUBREY – 1664

MUSGRAVE – 1718

APPROXIMATE SCALE OF FEET.

DONNE – 1769

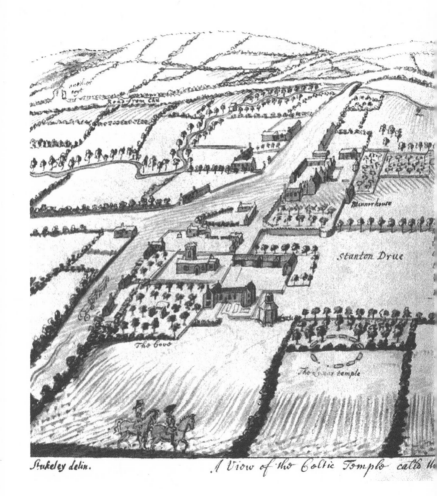

Stukeley delin.

Manorhouse

Stanton Drue

The boue

The water temple

A View of the Celtic Temple call'd the

# An Overview of the Site
## *the megalithic complex*

...ton Drew consists of three stone circles, the most prominent, ...wn as the Great Circle, being one of the largest stone circles in ...ain. With a diameter of approx 112m (367.5ft) and an area of some ...o square metres (6562ft), it is second only in size to Avebury, and, ...its sister temple in Wiltshire, was originally approached by an ...ue of standing stones.

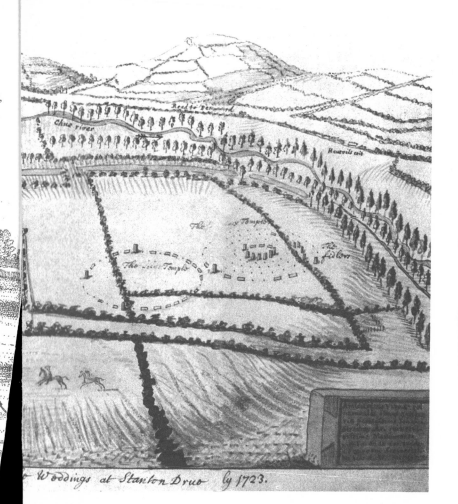

...o Weddings at Stanton Drew by 1723.

# QUARRYING
## *and transporting the stones*

The stones that make up the three circles of Stanton Drew were probably quarried a few miles away, from the site at Rudge Hill in West Harptree. Possibly the various colours and shapes of the stones were chosen by those who selected them at the quarry, and that this is what gives them their singular character.

Indeed, they are all individual, each one with its own personality. Some have flat tops, some pointed tops, characteristics that perhaps might be interpreted as 'lunar' and 'solar', and interestingly the custom of finishing the top of a stone wall in this manner is still common in Somerset. It is a style known as 'cock and hen'.

The proliferation of megalithic structures worldwide in the Neolithic period has led to keen debate as to how these immense stones were transported over such vast distances. The stones of Stanton Drew are relatively small compared to the giants of Avebury and Stonehenge, but to transport them five miles would none the less have demanded great determination and ingenuity. The most broadly accepted explanation with regard to the Stanton Drew stones is that they were transported by raft along the River Chew, whose course follows the northern edge of the site.

Other suggested means of transport have included rollers, levers, levitation and even teleportation!

*Lower opposite: An 1850s view of Carnac, France, showing locals in front of the menhirs.*

*Above: Brick-making near Stanton Drew, 1798. Smaller sto...*

The two other circles are situated to the north-east and south-west respectively, the Northeast Circle being 29.6m (97ft) in diameter, and the Southwest Circle 42m (138ft). The Southwest Circle is aligned to a standing stone situated to the north of the site known as Hauteville's Quoit, while a group of three stones known as the Cove can be found in the garden of the village pub. It is thought that the Cove may once have been a cromlech (an arrangement like a table).

# THE THIRD TEMPLE
*sibling of Stonehenge and Avebury*

Although often regarded as a minor megalithic site, there is now evidence that Stanton Drew predates both Stonehenge and Avebury. In fact techniques of henge-building used at Avebury and Stonehenge might have been developed first at Stanton Drew. This ancient Somerset site might have originally served a huge catchment area stretching down to Cornwall and across to Wiltshire.

Theories about the site abound. One of most endearing of the antiquarians to study Stanton Drew was Ernest Sibree (1859-1927), lecturer in Oriental studies at the University of Bristol in the late nineteenth and early twentieth centuries. From his cosmological studies, Sibree concluded that the purpose of Stanton Drew was a planetary calendar. Aided by the research of Dymond, who described the circles as 'peristaliths', Sibree postulated that the stones were used to calculate the passing of a year.

VIEW OF N.E. CIRCLE, LOOKING W.

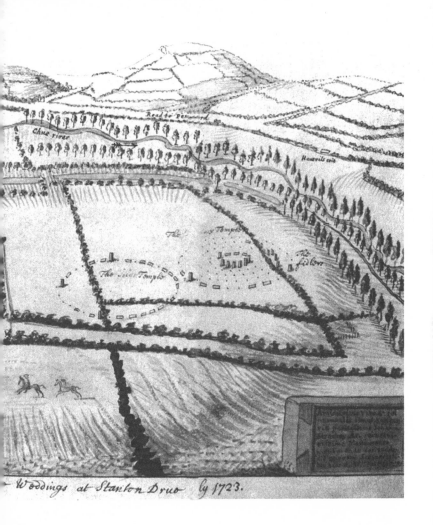

Weddings at Stanton Drue by 1723.

# QUARRYING
## and transporting the stones

The stones that make up the three circles of Stanton Drew were probably quarried a few miles away, from the site at Rudge Hill in West Harptree. Possibly the various colours and shapes of the stones were chosen by those who selected them at the quarry, and that this is what gives them their singular character.

Indeed, they are all individual, each one with its own personality. Some have flat tops, some pointed tops, characteristics that perhaps might be interpreted as 'lunar' and 'solar', and interestingly the custom of finishing the top of a stone wall in this manner is still common in Somerset. It is a style known as 'cock and hen'.

The proliferation of megalithic structures worldwide in the Neolithic period has led to keen debate as to how these immense stones were transported over such vast distances. The stones of Stanton Drew are relatively small compared to the giants of Avebury and Stonehenge, but to transport them five miles would none the less have demanded great determination and ingenuity. The most broadly accepted explanation with regard to the Stanton Drew stones is that they were transported by raft along the River Chew, whose course follows the northern edge of the site.

Other suggested means of transport have included rollers, levers, levitation and even teleportation!

*Lower opposite: An 1850s view of Carnac, France, showing locals in front of the menhirs.*

*Above: Brick-making near Stanton Drew, 1798. Smaller stones for modern times.*

# An Overview of the Site
## *the megalithic complex*

Stanton Drew consists of three stone circles, the most prominent, known as the Great Circle, being one of the largest stone circles in Britain. With a diameter of approx 112m (367.5ft) and an area of some 2,000 square metres (6562ft), it is second only in size to Avebury, and, like its sister temple in Wiltshire, was originally approached by an avenue of standing stones.

The two other circles are situated to the north-east and south-west respectively, the Northeast Circle being 29.6m (97ft) in diameter, and the Southwest Circle 42m (138ft). The Southwest Circle is aligned to a standing stone situated to the north of the site known as Hauteville's Quoit, while a group of three stones known as the Cove can be found in the garden of the village pub. It is thought that the Cove may once have been a cromlech (an arrangement like a table).

# THE THIRD TEMPLE
## *sibling of Stonehenge and Avebury*

Although often regarded as a minor megalithic site, there is now evidence that Stanton Drew predates both Stonehenge and Avebury. In fact techniques of henge-building used at Avebury and Stonehenge might have been developed first at Stanton Drew. This ancient Somerset site might have originally served a huge catchment area stretching down to Cornwall and across to Wiltshire.

Theories about the site abound. One of most endearing of the antiquarians to study Stanton Drew was Ernest Sibree (1859-1927), lecturer in Oriental studies at the University of Bristol in the late nineteenth and early twentieth centuries. From his cosmological studies, Sibree concluded that the purpose of Stanton Drew was a planetary calendar. Aided by the research of Dymond, who described the circles as 'peristaliths', Sibree postulated that the stones were used to calculate the passing of a year.

VIEW OF N.E. CIRCLE, LOOKING W.

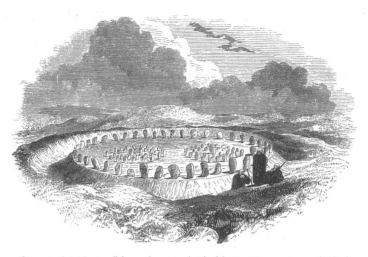

*Opposite: C. W. Dymond's late 19th century sketch of the site. Stanton Drew is the third largest temple of Southern Britain, after Avebury (above) and Stonehenge (below).*

# A GREAT HENGE
## *surrounding the site*

An enormous henge ditch, 135m in diameter and 7m wide, once encompassed the main circle at Stanton Drew with an opening to the north-east, perhaps allowing sight of the Midsummer sunrise. During excavations several pits were also found, five in the central area of the rings and four in the NE Circle, in a quadrilateral pattern aligning with opposing pairs of the eight stones of that circle. The pits may have contained posts or stones which were removed, possibly an earlier smaller version of the present monument.

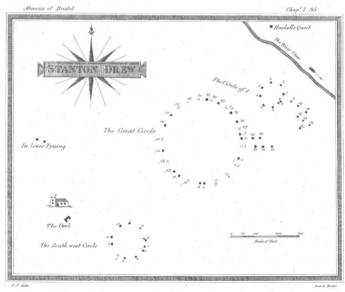

B.R.Baker Lithog.                                                    Printed by C.Hullmandel

VIEW OF STONES AT STANTON DREW.

# THE WOODEN BUILDING
## *before the stones*

Possibly contemporary with the henge ditch enclosure, on the site of what would later become the Great Circle, stood a massive woodhenge, larger and older than the examples at either Avebury or Woodhenge. When originally constructed, four to five hundred oak pillars, probably a metre (3.28ft) in diameter and 26 feet in height, and each weighing 5 tons, occupied an area about the size of a football field. They were set in nine concentric circles, a highly symbolic number (there are nine worlds in many ancient cosmologies), and would likely have been carved or decorated.

This sophisticated structure was discovered in 1997 by the English Heritage geophysical survey and could easily have accommodated a thousand people if not more, suggesting its use as a possible focal point for social or religious gatherings. A common theory is that the site might have been dedicated to funerary ritual, but a host of other explanations have been put forward.

Britain boasts many other woodhenge sites (or timber temples, as some authorities quaintly refer to them), including Balfarg in Fife, Scotland and Mount Pleasant in Dorset and the Seahenge site on the Norfolk coast, but Stanton Drew is the largest of them all.

The woodhenge was eventually replaced by the stones of the Great Circle, a similar story to the Sanctuary at Avebury, where a stone circle still stood in Stukeley's day replacing the original roundhouse there. Whether the stones formed part of the original woodhenge design or came later still remains to be established.

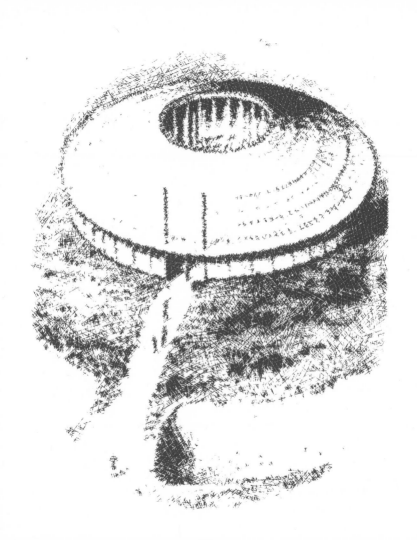

# THE STONE CIRCLES
## *megalithic magic*

---

The stones at Stanton Drew are the final characters to play on the stage. Replacing the wooden structure, the stone megaliths might have neatly filled the spaces between the wooden posts and the ditch that made up the original construction, we do not yet know if they were contemporary.

Today, Stanton Drew's most famous feature is undoubtedly its stones. At the monument's heart is the Great Circle which, like Stonehenge, originally consisted of some 30 stone giants, of whom an impressive 27 still survive. Indeed, the Great Circle at Stanton Drew is one of the largest and most impressive stone circles in the world, and easily dwarfs the two accompanying circles that complete the ancient site. Like the Northeast Circle, the Great Circle was once approached by an avenue of standing stones, although many of these have since fallen. What remains of a second avenue still meets the Great Circle from the north-east.

Although today in ruin, megalithic monuments such as Stanton Drew still evoke in many visitors a considerable degree of spiritual upliftment, mystical stirring, even awe. But perhaps the real magic is in the incredible feat accomplished by our ancestors in the construction of these ancient marvels, utilizing little more than a keen desire and a system of technological wizardry unsurpassed since. With careful alignments, as we shall see, to the heavens, and utilising complex geometries, they created monuments which have lasted over 4,000 years. No cement or mortar required.

B. R. Baker Lithog.                                    Printed by C. Hullmandel

VIEW OF STONES AT STANTON DREW.

# VIEWS OF STANTON DREW
## *entering the sacred place*

Although the stones of the Great Circle run outside where the timber circles once stood, they none the less fall within the circumference of the henge ditch. This might suggest that the woodhenge was visible when the stones were erected. It is certainly possible that the two structures were contemporary.

The idea of 'accessibility' associated with stone circles is also of interest here. The complex design of the woodhenge, with the possibility of 'screens' or 'panels' obscuring the view between the uprights, suggests a closed, exclusive function. This contrasts dramatically with the public nature of most stone circles.

The drawings below and opposite by Dan Goodfellow are accurate copies of three sketches of Stanton Drew from 1784 and show the site when there were more trees growing.

# HAUTEVILLE'S QUOIT
## *another megalithic mystery*

The most northerly feature of the complex, Hauteville's Quoit, gained its name from the 13th century crusader, Sir John Hauteville who, legend tells, was bigger and stronger than any man of his time. It is said he hauled three stout men to the top of nearby Norton Tower, one under each arm, the third between his teeth. Having reached the crest of the hill he "heaved up a mighty stone of thirty tons in weight and flung it a distance of more than a mile" towards Stanton Drew. Today the stone lies recumbent near Hauteville Quoit Farm, barely half its original size—over the years chunks of the stone have been broken off and used for mending the roads.

*Above: The fallen Quoit of the Whispering Knights, near the Rollright Stones, Oxfordshire*

*Left: William Barnes' 19th century woodcut, said to be of Hauteville's Quoit. Barnes' woodcuts are notoriously inaccurate.*

*Below: Chun Quoit in West Cornwall, from Borlase's Naenia Cornubiae, 1871. A fine example of a dolmen or quoit, with it's capstone still in place. No good explanation for these enigmatic structures has ever been put forward. They continue to vex archaeologists to this day.*

# THE COVE
*irregular stones in the distance*

The Cove (derived from Old English *cofa*, an alcove, and from the ancient German for hollow place) is situated in the garden of the Druids Arms public house a short distance from the main site. Tradition has a shaman occupying the place and receiving messages from the gods. Consisting of two still-standing stones with one recumbent slab separating them, all three of varying sizes, the stones of the Cove are mineralogically diverse from the stones comprising the circles, perhaps suggesting a different construction date.

The Cove is situated on an alignment that passes through nearby St. Mary's Church and extends through the centre of the Great Circle to the centre of the Northeast Circle.

*Opposite: The Avebury Cove, where the third stone is fallen, from William Stukeley's book of 1743. This page, clockwise from top left: late 19th century drawings of the Cove at Stanton Drew by C. W. Dymond's, William Barnes and H. M. J. Underhill. Coves are thought to indicate lunar extremes, but the Stanton Drew example, which points south, seems to contradict this. Overleaf: The Stanton Drew Cove, from William Stukeley's Itinerarium Curiosum, 1724.*

# UNEXPLAINED
## *the enigma of the megaliths*

It is interesting to bear in mind just how little we understand about quite what our Neolithic ancestors were really up to, and it can be equally interesting to study society's reactions to new pieces of the jigsaw when they appear. The function of coves is but one example. Another, taken at random might be cursuses. These enormous structures, of which 150 are known in the UK (*see Stukeley's plates of the Stonehenge Cursus shown below*), can date back to 4,000 BC, making them among the oldest monumental building works in the world. From six miles long (the Dorset Cursus) to less than half a mile, they could have been Neolithic racecourses, fairgrounds, ritual processional pathways, or, as has been suggested, flying saucer landing runways. The truth is we simply do not know.

And why did the builders of stone circles go to such incredible lengths to incorporate complex geometry and astronomy into their sites, often extending miles into the distance, with complicated geometrical axes indicating sites far away? And what are the mysterious energies which people say they feel at these places. Are they real, or imagined? Did our ancestors have subtle perceptions now lost to all but a few? The truth is we do not know.

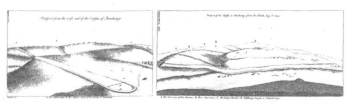

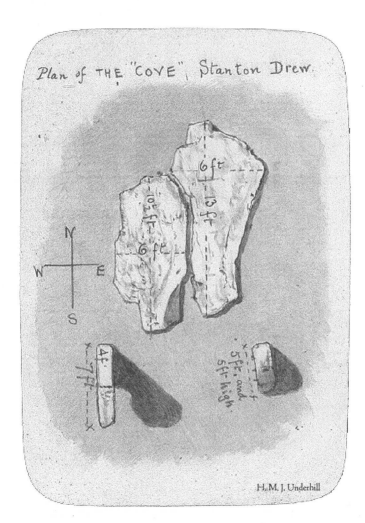

Plan of THE "COVE", Stanton Drew.

6 ft

10½ ft

13 ft

6 ft

N
W — E
S

4 ft

7 ft

5 ft. and
5 ft. high

H. M. J. Underhill

# ALIGNMENTS
## *ley-hunting at Stanton Drew*

Ley-lines (alignments of ancient sites over distance) appear to be evident around Stanton Drew. A line running from the Cove, for example, passes through St. Mary's church, on to the Great Circle and to the centre of the Northeast Circle.

A longer ley line runs from the church to the Iron Age fort at Dolebury Camp and then on to Brean Down. Yet another is said to pass through the stones at the ancient settlement at Cameley (linked with the Knights Templar and the Holy Grail) on its way to Maes Knoll and subsequently to the Market Cross in the old city centre of Bristol. Dundry Down and Cadbury Camp (at Tickenham) are also thought to be aligned with Stanton Drew.

Importantly, from the centre of the Great Circle the midsummer sunrise in 2,000 BC would have been at the point where Hauteville's Quoit is located, on an alignment that passes through the exact centre of the Great Circle to the centre of the SW Circle (*opposite top*).

On a flat plain midsummer sunrise will exactly oppose midwinter sunset, but at Stanton Drew, due to the lie of the land, the midwinter sunset in 2,000 BC from the centre of the Great Circle would have aligned with the Cove, on a line back through the centre of the Great Circle to the NE Circle. This midwinter line is at a bearing which suggests a hidden pentagonal geometry as it is defined by a pentagram pointing due east (the traditional geomantic orientation of a pentagram or pentagon in the landscape). The midsummer line is similarly defined as five-ninths of the way round from North.

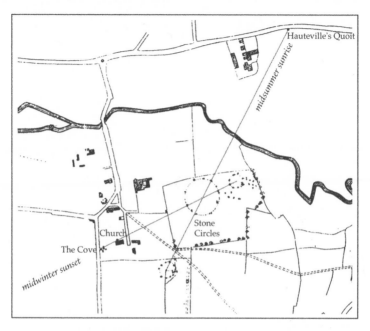

Hauteville's Quoit

midsummer sunrise

Stone
Circles

Church

The Cove

midwinter sunset

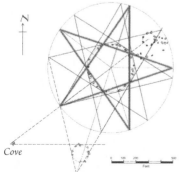

N

Cove

0    100    200         500
Feet

*Above:  Schematic diagram showing
midsummer sunrise and midwinter  sunset
alignments as defined by the geometry of
the primary elements at Stanton Drew.*

*Left:  Diagram by J. Martineau showing
the 144-degree pentagonal angle created
by the midwinter sunset line.*

# GEOMETRY OF THE CIRCLES
## triangles & octagons

It was C. W. Dymond, in his 1877 essay *Megalithic Monuments at Stanton Drew*, who first noticed the edge alignment between the three circles of the monument (*shown as a dotted line in the diagram lower opposite*). Little did he realise at the time what he had stumbled upon, for it was not until the 20th century, with Alfred Watkins' perception that edge-alignments are common in Neolithic alignments, and the astroarchaeological discovery that the edge alignment at Stanton Drew also marks the southernmost moonset from the site, that the full importance of this piece of the jigsaw began to be appreciated. Another important relationship present at Stanton Drew is a northerly edge-alignment (*shown as a dotted line opposite top*), almost identical to the layout of the Avebury henge relative to the position of Silbury Hill.

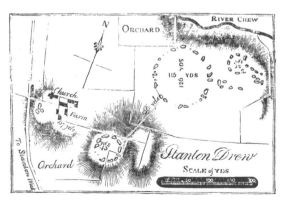

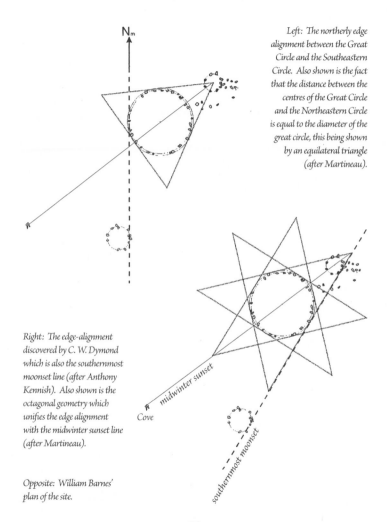

N<sub>m</sub>

*Left: The northerly edge alignment between the Great Circle and the Southeastern Circle. Also shown is the fact that the distance between the centres of the Great Circle and the Northeastern Circle is equal to the diameter of the great circle, this being shown by an equilateral triangle (after Martineau).*

*Right: The edge-alignment discovered by C. W. Dymond which is also the southernmost moonset line (after Anthony Kennish). Also shown is the octagonal geometry which unifies the edge alignment with the midwinter sunset line (after Martineau).*

*Opposite: William Barnes' plan of the site.*

midwinter sunset

Cove

southernmost moonset

# VANISHED STONES
## *the lost megaliths*

A number of stones from the original design of Stanton Drew are today sadly missing. Specific references are made in the nineteenth century, for example, to 'Tyning's Stones', a pair of megaliths in a field called Middle Ham at Lower Tyning, aligned due West of the Great Circle (*see page vi*). Both were reportedly over 5ft in height, but local sources tell of these two megaliths having been removed in the 1960s. Regrettably, like the Tollhouse Stone (*see page 3*), no trace of them remains.

Other stories relate that further stones, particularly from the Great Circle, were destroyed in the Medieval period, and in the eighteenth century many were reportedly lost to masonry and road metalling. The later use of Stoney Close (the area containing the Great Circle and the Northeast Circle) as an orchard and for various kinds of farming, would no doubt have caused even further damage. Thus, sadly, some of the original giants of Stanton Drew no longer grace this magnificent site.

Despite these trials, however, a good many of the stones of the great circle remain where they fell. A little poking around with a stick on a wet afternoon will enable the keener visitor to discover the outline of some veritable monsters lying just under the turf. Other stones are overgrown but visible. As with Arbor Low, in Derbyshire, one wonders why these fantastic sites are not properly restored and their stones re-erected. Perhaps the authorities are frightened of the magic that might be unleashed if they were.

## ESTIMATED ORIGINAL NUMBER OF STONES IN THE CIRCLES.

|  | MUSGRAVE | STUKELEY | WOOD | RUTTER | WILKINSON | DYMOND |
|---|---|---|---|---|---|---|
| S.W. Circle ... | — | 12 | 12 | 12 | 18 | 12 |
| Great Circle ... | 32 | 30 | 81 | 30 | 38 | 30 at least |
| N.E. Circle ... | — | 9 | 8 | 7 | — | 8 |

## DIAMETERS OF CIRCLES.

|  | STUKELEY | WOOD | COLLINSON | SEYER | CROCKER | WILKINSON | DYMOND |
|---|---|---|---|---|---|---|---|
| S.W. Circle ... | 120 | 140 | — | — | 129 | 130 | 145 |
| Great Circle ... | 300 | 378 | 300 | 342 | 378 × 345 | 380 × 347 | 368 |
| N.E. Circle ... | 90 | 96 | 84 | 94 to 96 | 96 | c. 96 | 97 |

Diameters in feet.

## DISTANCES BETWEEN GROUPS.

|  | WOOD | DYMOND |  | WOOD | DYMOND |
|---|---|---|---|---|---|
| Cove to S.W. Circle ... | — | 541.6 | Great Circle to N.E. Circle | 375 | 379.8 |
| Cove to Great Circle ... | 992 | 988.0 | Great Circle to Quoit ... | c. 1860 | c. 1856 |
| S.W. Circle to Great Circle | 714 | 711.6 | Great Circle to Two Stones | — | c. 3305 |

Distances in feet and inches, from centre to centre.

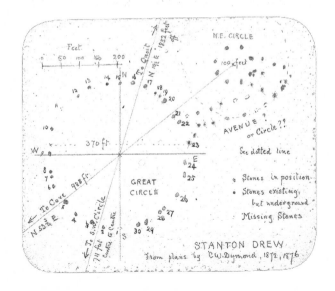

STANTON DREW
From plans by C.W. Dymond, 1872, 1876.

# MYSTERIOUS FORCES
## *light phenomena at the stones*

Major F.A.Menzies, a distinguished First World War Army engineer and surveyor, claimed he witnessed unusual phenomena at Stanton Drew in the 1940s. Having moved to France to study Feng Shui, he was an established geomancer, reportedly able to locate ley lines and advise on ill health caused by geopathic stress. One day, he had an extraordinary experience which was later related to fellow surveyor, George Sandwich in 1952, a year before his death:

S.J.Lorton

*"Although the weather was dull there was no sign of a storm. Just at a moment when I was re-checking a bearing on one of the stones in that group, it was as if a powerful flash of lightning hit the stone, so the whole group was flood-lit, making them glow like molten gold in a furnace. Rooted to the spot – unable to move – I became profoundly awestruck, as dazzling radiations from above caused the whole group of stones to pulsate with energy in a way that was terrifying. Before my eyes, it seemed the stones were enveloped in a moving pillar of fire – radiating light without heat – writhing upwards towards the heavens: on the other hand it was descending in a vivid spiral effect of various shades of colour – earthward. In fact the moving, flaring lights gyrating around the stones had joined the heavens with the earth."*

# DOWSING STANTON DREW
## *ways to the beyond*

The dowsers' surveys on these pages were rescued off a bonfire by a Mr Ali Carr in 1990 and kindly made available for this book. They are the previously unpublished maps of the telluric looping and spiralling 'aquastats' and 'influence lines' around Stanton Drew made by the legendary dowser Guy Underwood of Bradford-on-Avon in the 1950s.

Many people can feel subtle energies at a powerful site like Stanton Drew, and each dowser tends to see these energies in their own particular way, but Guy Underwood perhaps did more to accurately record the fine details of his dowsings than any twigger before or since. With his own patented dowsing rod, Underwood discovered that energies at sacred sites work in ways we can scarcely imagine.

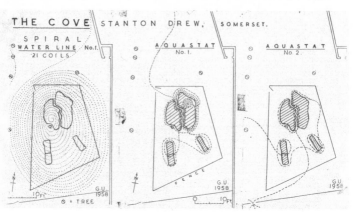

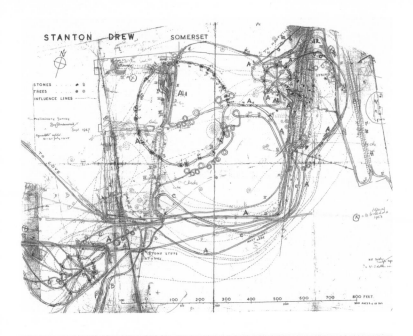

STANTON DREW — SOMERSET

STONES
TREES
INFLUENCE LINES

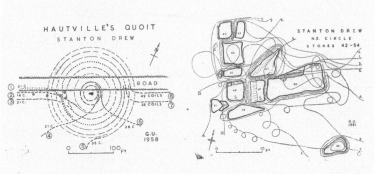

HAUTVILLE'S QUOIT
STANTON DREW

ROAD

49 COILS
35 COILS

G.U.
1958

0    100 FT.

STANTON DREW
N.E. CIRCLE
STONES 42 – 54

G.U.
1951

0    10 FT.

39

# STONEY LITTLETON
## and other local sites

If you are visiting Stanton Drew then nine miles to the southeast is another Neolithic site well worth a look. Archaeologist James Dyer describes the Stoney Littleton long barrow as "the most notable chambered long-barrow in south-western England". Located at Wellow near Bath, Stoney Littleton has seven individual chambers, with the central passage orientated to capture the rising sun at the Winter Solstice. Superbly positioned with a high vantage point over the surrounding countryside, its atmosphere, particularly at the time of the full moon, can only be described as 'electric'.

About 30m (98.4ft) in length and 15m (49.2ft) wide at the south-east end, it stands nearly 3m (9.84ft) high. There is a horned entrance with a fossilised ammonite cast on the western door-jamb (*clearly visible in Dan Goodfellow's drawing, right*), while the entrance leads to a gallery 16m (52.5ft) long, but only 1m (3.28ft) high.

Several long barrows are also found near Stanton Drew, in the nearby Mendip Hills. The Fairy Toot (or Tit because of its mammary shape) may have been named after Thoth, whose name it is thought was pronounced 'Tot'. Although now mostly destroyed, this could have been a 'moot' place where the clans congregated.

Other sites of interest include the Priddy henges and barrows up on the Mendip hills (*next page*), the Pen Hill long barrow, just north of Wells, and the Deerleap stones near Ebbor Gorge. Old OS maps show a landscape full of ancient sites in the Somerset and Avon landscape, suggesting this was a well populated and thriving area.

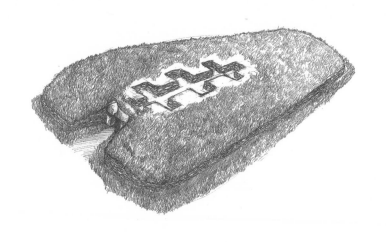

41

# THE NEOLITHIC VISION
## *and the Priddy Circles*

The original earth structures at Stanton Drew are thought to date back as far as the Middle Neolithic period (c. 3,500 BC). Whether a direct connection between megalithic structures and the transition from nomadic hunter-gatherer to the more settled late Stone Age farmer can be absolutely established remains open to debate, but never before or since this seminal age in human prehistory have such remarkable structures been built.

Some scholars argue that the mature science of megalithic architecture arrived in Britain with the 'Beakers', a Bronze Age race who migrated from northern France circa 3000 BC. The Beaker people, renowned for their craftsmanship and so-called because they buried beakers with their dead, were known to have built stone monuments prior to their migration to Britain. Their subsequent integration with late Neolithic Britons is thus thought to have sparked the revolution in human technology responsible for the great stone temples of Stonehenge, Avebury and Stanton Drew.

*Above: Cistvaen on Dunry Hill, and the entrance to Stoney Littleton Longbarrow, by William Barnes*

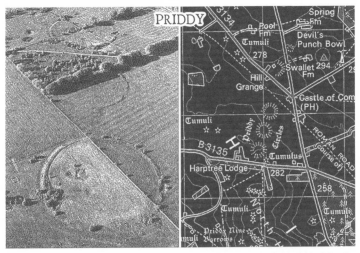

*Three ancient sites of Southern Britain which all mysteriously display a 19½° tilt (also the 'wake' angle behind an object moving through water). Above: the Priddy henges, exactly southwest of Stanton Drew. Below: Avebury, and Lockyer's 1905 astronomical survey of the Hurlers on Bodmin Moor (after Martineau).*

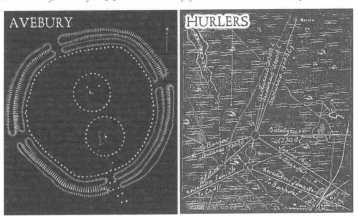

43

# LEGEND AND HEALING
## *spirit of the stones*

A legend attached to Stanton Drew tells of how the stone circles were formed when a party of wedding guests and their fiddlers were turned to stone as punishment for allowing the Devil to fool them into extending their Saturday night revels beyond midnight, and into Sunday morning: the Sabbath. When dawn broke, everybody had been turned to stone: thus the stone circles are the petrified dancers, the avenues are the fiddlers, and the Cove is the bride and the groom with the drunken churchman at their feet. This same tale is attached to various stone circles throughout the land: the Hurlers, the Merry Maidens, the Nine Maidens and numerous others.

Another feature of the site, shared with Long Meg and Her Daughters and many other megalithic monuments, states that the Stanton Drew stones are uncountable. In 1750, it is said that John Wood tried to count the stones, but immediately a thunderstorm broke out, preventing him from completing the task. Another superstition relates how, on the sixth day of the full moon, at midnight, the stones walk down to the River Chew to get a drink. Beware getting in their way!

There are other magical stories related to stone circles, not least that the stones possess inherent curative properties. Hence the superstition of climbing through stone rings in order to be healed. Some say this is due to the presence of quartz, which in some form or another appears in every kind of rock used in the construction of megalithic monuments. Indeed the tradition of using quartz in healing and initiatory ceremonies is very ancient indeed.

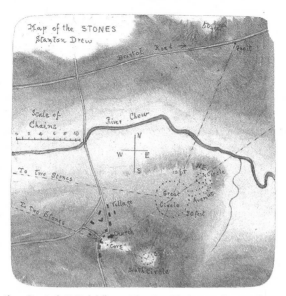

*Above: Drawing by H. Underhill, 1895. Below: Cornish healing stone, from Bottrell, 1870*

# RITUAL AT THE STONES
*who knows what went on*

Although not widely discussed in learned volumes there are other possible interpretations of sites like Stanton Drew, and from dim records of ancient customs it seems quite possible that human sacrifices or rituals of a sexual nature may have taken place there with the purpose of evoking a symbolic union, either between life and death, or man and woman. Again unmentionable in the hallowed halls of academia is the high likelihood that those taking part in such rituals may have been in an altered state of consciousness. Ergot, deadly nightshade, henbane, fly-agaric and liberty cap mushrooms, marijuana and opiates were all available to our Neolithic ancestors and significant deposits of mid-altering substances have been found in British burial mounds. It is therefore not unreasonable to conclude that initiates may have been 'high' at ceremonies.

The contemporary equivalent is a popular festival. Chanting, drumming and the wailing of pipes would provide the musical element and mind-expanding substances would leaven the spiritual brew. It is possible that drugs, with all of the enhanced perceptions they can bring, may have been as much part of the lifestyle of 4,000 BC as they are today.

Perhaps the hippy dream of enlightenment and 'turning on' had its inception way back then. Echoes survive today at nearby Priddy with its folk fairs and ample supply of 'magic mushrooms'—a popular rendezvous for those who gather in our own age.

# THE DRUIDS
## *keepers of the stones*

Despite Stukeley's promotion of the Druids as guardians of Stonehenge, as well as other sites such as Avebury and Stanton Drew, there is no direct evidence to connect the Celtic Druids with circle monuments. Indeed, tradition maintains they performed their sacred rites in groves, caves and remote valleys.

The problem with associating Druids with megalithic monuments has always been that the first henges were constructed in Britain as far back as circa 3,700 BC, and until now we have assumed that the Celts did not arrive in Britain until much later. More recently, however, academic opinion has shifted.

A relatively new school of thought now postulates that the Celtic 'invasion', dated at around 500 BC, never actually happened. Experts now tend to agree that the origin of the so-called 'Celtic tribes' is more complex than first presumed, and some historians now place the earliest Celtic migrants in Britain as early as 2,000 BC. Certainly it is now accepted that the Celts might have migrated to Britain over a period of some centuries rather than having 'invaded' the isles on one particular Saturday afternoon in 500 BC.

This hypothesis, of course, makes it possible that the priestly caste of the Celts, the Druids, might have lived in Britain much earlier than previously believed. And thus that they might indeed boast a closer association with stone circles than originally thought.

# GODS AND GODDESSES
*spirit of place*

When trying to understand the complex religious or ritual psychology of the ancient Neolithic Briton, it can help to look across the waves to that other great culture of the same millennium, ancient Egypt. The common notion of the initiate giving up his earthly life to become divine has its origins among the sacrificial gods—in Egypt Osiris represented the divine element in man, and his ritual murder, dismemberment and resurrection was enacted as a magical depiction of the fertile power of nature and the cycle of the agricultural year. The Egyptian Sun God Horus was traditionally born at midwinter, signalling the return of the Sun, a date immortalised in stone at Stanton Drew.

Thoth, also Lugh, Mercurial God of the Underworld had his festival (Lugnasadh or Lammas) on August 1st, halfway between midsummer and the autumn equinox. Ancient texts advise students to look for him where the mountains meet the sky, at dusk when night meets day and on the shoreline where land meets water.

In fact, whatever route you take in life to make sense of the miracle of conscious life on Earth, Britain's ancient sites, Stanton Drew among them, stand in testimony to the fact that you are not alone in pondering such things. As you walk about the crystal-studded stones, enjoy the view, the air, and the sense of great antiquity, it is humbling to realise just how little we really know about our ancestors.

If only the stones could speak. Or perhaps they can, it is just we who have forgotten how to listen.

56.—The Druid Grove.

# THE SONG OF STANTON DREW
*they danced and they danced*

Midsummer eve it fell on a Saturday
  Sue and William went to be wed
They had music played by a fiddler'
  "Let's go dancing!" William said.

They danced and danced and danced around
  They danced and danced to the fiddler's sound
They danced with a skip, they danced with a hop,
  It seemed that nothing could make them stop.

Midnight struck and then said the fiddler
  "Dancing on a Sunday wouldn't be right,"
Sue gave a laugh, "Don't care if to Hell I go
  I'll find another fiddler tonight."

They danced and danced and danced around
  They danced and danced to the fiddler's sound
They danced with a skip, they danced with a hop,
  It seemed that nothing could make them stop.

Off went the fiddler, left them all grumbling,
  Then another fiddler came along the way.
"You'd like to dance and I'd like to play for you"
  Tunes he played both merry and gay.

They danced and danced and danced around
  They danced and danced to the fiddler's sound

They danced with a skip, they danced with a hop,
  It seemed that nothing could make them stop.

"Stop" cried the dancers, "NO" cried the fiddler,
  He kept on in spite of their moans.
They couldn't stop their jerking and a stumbling,
  Then in a flash, he turned them into stones.

They danced and danced and danced around
  They danced and danced to the fiddler's sound
They danced with a skip, they danced with a hop,
  It seemed that nothing could make them stop.

Stanton Drew in the County of Somerset
  That's where the Devil played at Sue's request,
They paid the price for dancing on a Sunday.
  Now they are standing evermore at rest.

*by Kim Ravenscroft (RIP)*

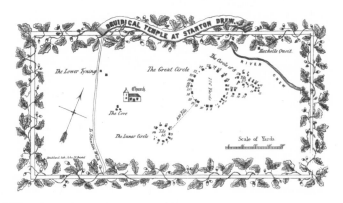

# NOTES

If the Great Circle is figured as the size of the Earth,
then the NE Moon Circle will be the size of the Moon
(very accurate indeed!) - Oliver Percival

*The octagonal NE Circle is really a Venus circle, with its
eight stones marking the eight years (and 99 full moons) of
the Venus pentagram cycle - M. Lundy*